of related interest

The Every Body Book
The LGBTQ+ Inclusive Guide for Kids
about Sex, Gender, Bodies, and Families
By Rachel E. Simon
Illustrated by Noah Grigni
ISBN 978 1 78775 173 6
eISBN 978 1 78775 174 3

It's Totally Normal!
An LGBTQIA+ Guide to Puberty,
Sex, and Gender
By Monica Gupta Mehta
and Ash Lily Mehta
Illustrated by Fox Fisher
ISBN 978 1 83997 355 0
eISBN 978 1 83997 356 7

Your Gender Book
Helping You Be You!
By Ben Pechey
ISBN 978 1 83997 610 0
eISBN 978 1 83997 611 7

The Every Body Book of Consent

An LGBTQIA-Inclusive Guide to Respecting Boundaries, Bodies, and Beyond

By Rachel E. Simon

Illustrated by Noah Grigni

Jessica Kingsley Publishers
London and Philadelphia

First published in Great Britain in 2024 by Jessica Kingsley Publishers
An imprint of John Murray Press

1

Front cover image source: Noah Grigni

Content warning: This book contains mentions of homophobia and transphobia.

A CIP catalogue record for this title is available from the British Library and the Library of Congress

ISBN 978 1 83997 683 4
eISBN 978 1 83997 684 1

Printed and bound in China by Leo Paper Products Ltd

Jessica Kingsley Publishers' policy is to use papers that are natural, renewable and recyclable products and made from wood grown in sustainable forests. The logging and manufacturing processes are expected to conform to the environmental regulations of the country of origin.

Jessica Kingsley Publishers
Carmelite House
50 Victoria Embankment
London EC4Y 0DZ

www.jkp.com

John Murray Press
Part of Hodder & Stoughton Ltd
An Hachette Company

A Note for the Grown-Ups

Welcome back, trusted adults! If you've come from "The Every Body Book", I hope some of this information sounds familiar. You've already prioritized continuing conversations about sex and sexuality with your loved ones, encouraged your children to come to you with their questions and feelings, and provided information and resources to help build shame-free knowledge.

If you're new here, welcome to you, too! I am a clinical psychotherapist and sexuality educator, and I'm so glad you've chosen to dive into this book on consent with me.

In "The Every Body Book of Consent", we are talking about consent across a broad spectrum of topics. Making sure our preteens and teens understand the nuances of consent means treating this array of topics as more than just a one-off conversation, otherwise, we won't be as effective in helping them think. Exploring specific examples of consent will help your young people develop respect and empathy for themselves and others, and it will help place them in the multiple possible roles in relationships when consent comes up.

We often think about consent in a sexual context, but the

more we connect consent to our everyday decision-making, communication, and interactions, the more comfort we can build as our preteens grow up, and consent becomes more intimate.

I encourage you to talk to your children about their body parts, trusted adults, gut feelings and body safety, their feelings and values, and how they make choices. With preteens especially, discussing lots of practice situations can help teach them how they can make choices and how their behaviors affect others.

Making sure that kids have enough autonomy to refuse a hug or kiss from family and friends, and even from you, is a powerful message of self-advocacy. Parents and caregivers can be great models for bodily autonomy by asking for and giving respect for boundaries.

It can be useful to refer to media to help facilitate discussion prompts in your family; what conversations are missing, what assumptions are made, who in this movie scene had agency, etc. Putting ourselves in others' shoes and strengthening our critical thinking and empathy muscles are crucial in consent education.

As with "The Every Body Book", this book is for all kinds of kids and families. I hope the language and concepts feel affirming, validating, and inclusive for families just like yours, and ones that are not. I hope it challenges you to think about your own values and remain curious about those of the young people in your life.

Chapter 1:
Consent? What's That?

This is a book about **consent**. Consent is a word that means permission. We can give permission to others, get permission from others, or agree to something that's happening to us or around us. Why does there need to be a whole book about consent? Well, it might seem like consent means a simple yes or a simple no when asking or being asked for permission.

It's more than just a yes or no. Consent is also about feeling safe in our bodies, about feeling as if we are free to say yes and no confidently, and having healthy relationships with ourselves and other people.

When we feel free to give consent, it means we make a choice with something called **agency**. Agency means we have the power to make our own choices. Agency can be a tricky thing— it turns out we can't always have agency when we want it, because some people in our society have more agency than others, depending on how much **power** they have.

There are different types of power. For example, parents and other adults sometimes make choices for kids, especially when they are in charge of safety. Our agency grows as we get older, and we are able to do more things in the world on our own. This lets us have even more choices. We also need certain information about what we are consenting to, or else we can't call it consent.

For example, if someone offers you a cookie, but you are allergic to peanuts, you may need to ask some questions so you can make an informed choice about accepting and eating that cookie. If the cookie is nut-free, and your body is hungry for a cookie, then yum!

Consent to one specific thing doesn't mean consenting to all things though. If you offer to share that cookie with a friend, that doesn't mean they get to eat your sandwich, too!

When we don't give our consent and someone does something to us instead of with us, that's **nonconsensual** (without our consent). If someone came up to you and started tickling you without asking, that would be nonconsensual. They don't even know if you like being tickled or not!

To see if something is consensual, an important question to ask yourself is "Am I saying yes because I actually want to say yes, or because I feel like I should?" Should can be a dangerous word when it comes to consent. If we feel pressured to make a certain choice because we feel like we should, we are not freely giving affirmative consent.

For example, have you ever said **yes** just to avoid hurting someone's feelings? It's important to consider how that might be taking away from our agency and feelings.

Consent, just like trust, isn't something you get from someone and have forever. You're allowed to want something one day, and then not want it the next day. You're even allowed to change your mind immediately! And if someone breaks your trust, you can change your mind about them, too.

We'll talk a lot in this book about your **network**, or group, of trusted adults. It's a good idea to have at least three adults, some of whom are not in your family, to rely on for help and safety. You might have questions or concerns about some of the things you read in this book.

It's a good idea to read this book with a trusted adult so you can talk about how some of these ideas can be useful in your everyday life. It also helps to be able to practice communication and consent with your trusted adults (see Chapter 3 for some special practice activities)!

Consent can be about little choices like "Do I want to let my sibling borrow my toy?" It can be about bigger choices like "Am I okay with my friend saying mean things to me?" It can be individual like "Do I want to wear my fuzzy jacket or my sparkly sweater today?" It can be relational with others like "Is this person someone I want as a friend?"

The decision to give consent involves a lot of self-reflection and getting to know your own values. You can self-reflect by asking yourself how a situation made you feel, and whether you would change anything about your decision-making in the future.

The values of **empathy**, **compassion**, and **respect** all relate to consent. Empathy means understanding other people's feelings. Compassion means concern for other people's feelings. Respect means considering and valuing other people's feelings.

It's also important to have respect, empathy, and compassion for ourselves! You can use the information in this book to consider all the ways you can work on practicing consent with yourself and with others.

Practice:

- greeting a family member
- ordering a pizza together
- waiting your turn and feeling impatient (delaying gratification, impulse control).

Chapter 2:
Your Body, Your Rules

You are the boss of your body! No one in the world is exactly the same as you. Some people might have the same body parts, or the same interests, or some of the same feelings as someone else, but you are the best expert on **you**. That's why it's important to know your own body and your boundaries.

Boundaries are limits, and they work as invisible lines between you and other people. You get to decide where those lines are, what gets to come in, and what has to stay out. One type of boundary is a physical or body boundary. Your body boundary is the space around your body, and people need to ask before they enter it. Some people call this your "personal space" or your "body bubble."

Body autonomy means that you get to decide, as the boss, what to do with your body and who's invited into your personal space. Body autonomy is something that everyone has. People should respect your choices for your body, and we should also respect theirs.

Another type of boundary is an emotional boundary. One example of an emotional boundary is having the right to have your own thoughts and feelings. Another example is that it's not okay to say hurtful things to people on purpose.

Our bodies can be really good at letting us know when something is starting to feel unsafe or not okay. We might feel a rumble in our bellies, or our hearts might beat faster. Sometimes we get those bodily feelings when we do something hard or exciting like riding a roller coaster or coasting down a hill on a bicycle. Other times these body feelings can be a warning that we do not feel safe.

It's important to check in with our bodies often, to see what they might be telling us. Your body's needs will change. Some days you need extra rest, and some days you have extra energy. Some days you crave a piece of pizza for lunch and some days you don't. Something that feels comfortable today isn't always going to feel comfortable tomorrow. Something that feels comfortable with one person might not feel comfortable with another.

We can call this our "gut feeling," our "instinct" or our "intuition," and it can help us understand what we're feeling and what we do (or don't) want. Our gut feelings can give us messages about feeling safe, cared for, comfortable, and loved. They can also give us messages about feeling uncomfortable. If your gut feelings are telling you that being with someone is scary, icky, or unsafe, it's a good idea to talk to one of your trusted adults.

There have probably been times when you didn't feel like the boss of your own body. Sometimes we have to hold someone's hand to cross the street, put a coat on when it's cold, or have our bodies checked at the doctor's office. These are situations where our trusted adults have to be the boss of keeping our bodies safe and healthy.

Even during safety, health, and hygiene tasks, it's okay to ask questions, press pause, and expect information about what's going to happen and when. You have the right to have a safe person with you at the doctor's office.

I know I have to get this shot, but will you tell me when to close my eyes?

Your body has private parts. They are the body parts covered by a bathing suit, like genitals (penises, testicles, and vulvas) and bottoms. None of those body parts are bad or shameful! They're parts that may need extra care, cleaning, and safety, and just like the rest of your body, they should never be touched without permission. Touching these body parts might feel good. If you want to explore your own body privately, alone in your own space, that's okay, and maybe even great!

Many kids have questions about their bodies and sex, especially as they change and grow. Talking about your body is important, and you can ask questions of your trusted adults, but remember, most people wouldn't bring up their sensitive body parts in front of a room full of people! That would be "in public," and we don't usually talk about sensitive body parts in public because not everyone is comfortable with the same conversations. Talking about bodies requires consent, too!

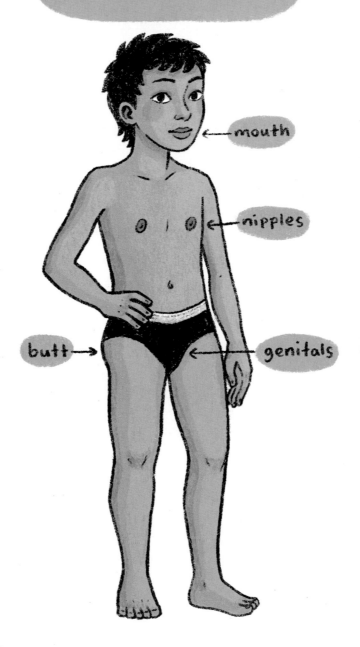

Special Section:
Diverse Minds and Bodies

There are many ways that bodies and minds can work, and that brings up even more important conversations about consent. About one in 2,000 babies have intersex traits, which means their bodies are not clearly male or female at birth. If you're an intersex person, you might have a combination of internal and external body parts that doctors might label "boy" or "girl."

Sometimes doctors and parents decide to change a baby's genitals to make them look or function like a more "typical" male or female body. Parents and doctors are often the ones who consent to these surgeries. Sometimes, there is a medical reason for surgery, like making sure a baby can pee properly. Other times, they are about how the baby's genitals look.

The problem is that parents and doctors don't have an important piece of information. Babies can't tell us their gender until they can use words, so parents and doctors don't know whether the baby will grow up to be a boy or a girl, or both, or neither. They try to guess for the baby, which means the baby is not able to consent to this decision about their body.

When surgery happens without consent, there can be many possible consequences. One of them is that people with intersex traits are unique individuals just like everyone else, and they may not be happy about having surgical decisions made for them without their consent. Many intersex activists and their allies speak out against these decisions and work to pass laws restricting surgery performed without consent.

There are other non-medical decisions that adults consent to for babies like circumcision of a baby's penis or piercing of a baby's ears. Some people disagree with those choices, too, and there is some debate about them.

Babies can't consent!

When we think about bodies and consent, we should also be thinking about disabled bodies. There are many ways to be in the world as a disabled person. Some disabilities require help that involves personal touching, which makes consent especially important since people should be able to say **yes** and **no** to being touched.

If you're someone who uses a wheelchair, for example, people might think they're helping by pushing you through the doorway. However, we should consider a wheelchair to be an extension of a person's body, and it shouldn't be touched without consent. You might prefer to move by yourself. The same thing goes for care tasks like helping a physically disabled person get dressed. Helpers should still ask before touching someone's body.

If someone has a type of intellectual disability that makes it hard to get verbal consent, it is still important to be as clear as possible with what you are asking and offering. Intellectual disabilities affect someone's ability to learn, think, and communicate verbally.

We can still pay attention to nonverbal (body) cues and respect the agency of people's bodies, even when helping care for them. If someone has a type of intellectual disability that makes it hard for them to understand **your** nonverbal cues, it's important to use clear verbal communication about what you want and need so they can understand your limits and boundaries.

It's important to remember that some people are neurodivergent, which means that their minds develop or work differently. For people who process information differently, we might need to consider the ways we communicate about consent.

For example, autism is a type of neurodivergence, and it might affect how you or someone you know processes information. Autistic people might not understand some nonverbal body language, sarcasm, or tone of voice.

Just like with neurotypical people, we should not assume that nonverbal communication is enough to proceed without clearer consent! It is important to understand sensory overload for autistic people too, which can cause communication shutdowns if someone is overwhelmed.

If someone communicates differently to you, you can work to learn each other's languages and cues so that you can both feel safe and understood.

Chapter 3:
Giving Consent and Getting Consent

There are lots of ways to say yes and no. Some of them are with exact words:

"Absolutely, I would love a hug and a kiss!"

"No, you cannot have a bite of this cookie."

"Okay sure, you can take a picture of me."

"Um, I don't want to dance right now."

Sometimes, people feel uncomfortable saying no. They might communicate no in a different way: "I'm not sure," showing some uncomfortable body language, or just not saying anything at all! This is one reason why it's important to **ask** for verbal consent, too,

Let's talk more about **verbal** and **nonverbal** consent. Verbal consent means you hear words like yes. Nonverbal consent is when you don't hear the words, but you can pay attention to other clues. Even babies who can't talk yet can show when they do and don't want to be hugged or held. If you've held a baby, think about what the baby liked and didn't like, and how the baby showed it.

You can practice this with friends, too! Start by noticing their faces, their body language, and their actions. Can you tell how they feel? You can always press pause on a game you're playing if someone looks uncomfortable (or if you're uncomfortable, too!). You can also have a code word that means "time out" or "stop," even if it's a silly word like "lobster." As long as everyone knows the word, it can be a great way to check in with one another.

Being with friends can help you pay attention to how people act in different situations, too. Sometimes, going along with the group can get in the way of making sure everyone is comfortable with what's going on. It's always a good idea to check in with your gut feelings and trust your knowledge about what's right and wrong.

We ask permission and give consent for lots of different kinds of things all the time. When it comes to sexual consent, this is especially important. Sexual consent means agreeing to participate in sexual activity, which is physical touch that is meant to create sexual pleasure. Sexual activity might include kissing, rubbing, stroking, and other stimulating touches, and can involve hands, mouths, genitals, chests, bottoms, and other body parts.

Sexual consent only works when everyone involved:

- can choose freely to say **yes** or no
- can change their minds at any time
- can say **yes** enthusiastically
- can understand what activities they are saying **yes** to
- is awake and not under the influence of drugs or alcohol
- is old enough to say **yes** according to the law.

Affirmative consent means that not only is someone okay with what you're doing, but they have clearly said **yes** and are actively participating. You can't tell if someone is consenting just by how they look, what they're wearing, what gender they are, whether they have consented to something before, or whether you are in a relationship with them.

Giving consent to one thing does not mean someone should assume you consent to another thing or all the things. If someone consents to you hugging them, this does not give you permission to kiss them, too. It also doesn't mean you always get to hug them whenever you want in the future.

If one person says yes and another person says no, the no always wins. It's important to respect a person's no and not try to convince them or pressure them to say yes instead. If everyone is comfortable talking about it later, you might be able to find out more about the no. You can ask the question: "Are you open to explaining your no, or do you want to stop talking about this?"

"No, I don't want to kiss you because I don't feel ready, but I would like to hold your hand if that's okay."

(It's also okay if no is the complete sentence.)

It's safer to ask someone what they're comfortable with instead of guessing based on their body cues or what we think they might want. Sexual consent is important for kissing, sexual touching, and sex of any kind.

Since sex can mean so many different things, someone needs to be as specific as possible with what they are asking to do. If someone says "okay" or "fine" to something but you're not sure how confident they are in their yes, it's important to check in. Sometimes people say yes because they think they're supposed to.

Sometimes they say yes because they're tired of saying no and not being heard. Sometimes they say yes to avoid making someone else upset. Sometimes they say yes because the person asking is older or has more power or authority. None of these types of yes are enthusiastic or confident. Consent is a yes that is free of pressure and free of fear.

All of these types of yes and no can be confusing for the person getting consent, and overwhelming for the person thinking about giving consent. This is why it's **so** important to pay attention, use very clear language, and check in with the other person.

Consent isn't about trying to get something you want from someone and hoping they let you have it. It's about real listening, so you only do things everyone wants with a free and confident yes. Every person has the right to choose to say yes or no for themselves.

Not everyone knows how to advocate for what they want. This is an important thing to practice and to help other people practice. Even if we're not in a culture that values consent and body autonomy, we can create that culture by saying loudly and clearly what our bodies want and need.

Chapter 4:
Boundary Setting + Respecting a No
= Healthy Communication

So, what if someone sets a boundary and says or communicates a no? Someone should only have to say no once, and it should be respected the first time.

What can you do if someone touches you without asking? You might say "No, respect my body boundary!" Then, you can tell them your boundary so they can respect it next time.

What can you do if you said yes but change your mind? You might say, "I changed my mind and I do not want this."

What if someone shares a joke that makes you feel uncomfortable? You might ask them not to tell those jokes around you anymore.

What if someone shares information about someone else who isn't there? You might say "Hey, that's private!"

Practice saying how you feel, what you want, and what you might say in a tough situation. Practice saying your enthusiastic yes and your clear no. Practice asking other people how they feel, what they want, and what their boundaries are.

Some people don't have the same information you do to practice consent. They might not have been taught that agency and body boundaries are important. Direct communication takes practice, and while you practice, you could be teaching others that their wants and needs are just as important as yours are.

Sometimes another person's boundary might not make sense to you. You might think that if you were in their position, you wouldn't make the same choice. It's okay to think about what choices you would make in different situations, but it's never okay to try to find your way around someone else's boundary.

Not everyone is the same, and it's okay if a friend says no to you. It might hurt your feelings, but it's their choice, and it doesn't mean they don't care about you.

It's OK if a friend says NO to you.

It's their choice to make, and it doesn't mean they don't care about you!

Even if we feel hurt or rejected, we need to show respect for others' boundaries, just as we deserve to have ours respected. It's okay to have hurt feelings, but we shouldn't use our hurt feelings to try to make someone change their choice.

It is okay to disappoint someone or be disappointed by someone. That's a part of being human. But rejection can really hurt! Here are three things you can do if you feel rejected:

- Give yourself space to reflect on your feelings.
- Remember you're a strong person who can make it through hard things.
- Talk to a trusted adult about what you're experiencing.

Here are three things you should not do if you feel rejected:

- Explode with anger at the person saying no.
- Feel guilty for asking at all.
- Refuse to accept someone else's no.

A note about sexual consent: Some people start having sexual feelings about others during puberty. Some people don't have sexual feelings until later on, some might have them sooner, and some don't have them at all!

Someone having sexual feelings or attraction to others doesn't always mean they want to act on them. Some people might want to explore their own bodies, and some people might not want to explore their own bodies. Touching your own body is your choice, and whether you're allowed to touch someone else's body is theirs!

Chapter 5:
Getting Support

You might be getting to an age where you care about your privacy more than ever before. Privacy can mean that you don't want anyone to see you change your clothes or use the bathroom. Privacy can also mean there's information about you that you don't want to share with just anyone.

Consent isn't just for bodies; it's for information, too! If someone shares our thoughts, our identities, our photos, or our private information without asking, it's nonconsensual.

Because people are not always safe or kind to LGBTQIA+ (lesbian, gay, bisexual, trans, queer, questioning, intersex, asexual, and more!) people, there are some special things about consent to think about. If someone tells you what pronouns they use, a very useful follow-up question might be "Are there any places or times when you want me to use different ones?" If someone tells you something about their identity, it is private information for your ears only, unless you have express permission to share that with others.

There is a difference between private information and secrets, and there's also a difference between secrets and surprises. If someone tells you private information about themselves, like their crush, their identity, or who is invited to their party, that's different from a harmful secret. That private information can help keep people feeling supported and safe.

Surprises can be fun, like a surprise party, gift, or a family trip! The difference is everyone will know about the surprise soon, and it's not forever.

Secrets can be trickier...you **should** tell your trusted adults if:

- an adult asks you to keep something secret
- someone is doing something dangerous
- someone is getting hurt
- someone is threatening to hurt themselves or others
- someone is being hateful
- someone has a dangerous object
- someone is lost or missing.

Bribes (someone offering you something in exchange for doing what they want) and threats ("if you don't do what I want, then I'll...") do not equal consent. Secrecy is not safe. If there is something unsafe happening, it's time to tell a trusted adult.

People make friends in all kinds of ways, on the internet and in person. It can feel really good to get to know someone new. One of the first things we do in a new friendship or relationship is work on building trust in a new person.

A lot of times when someone works hard to make you feel special and gain your trust, it's a wonderful step toward having a healthy relationship. But there are also some people out there who might take time to build your trust and then use it to behave in bad or unsafe ways, like asking you to keep secrets, keeping you away from safer people, and trying to touch you. They might use whatever power they have to threaten you not to tell anyone else. The name for this is **grooming**, and it's not safe at all.

If this happens to you, it's not your fault and it's important to talk to a trusted adult. If that trusted adult doesn't listen, keep telling and telling until you find one who does. You can tell someone at home, someone at school, a doctor or nurse, or anyone else who will listen.

Healthy relationships involve lots of body autonomy, safety, communication, and space for consent. Healthy relationships are ones where you can feel confident and respected, instead of scared to ask for what you need. Trustworthy people do not ask you to keep secrets, make threats, or try to control your behavior.

If you or someone you know is in an unhealthy or unsafe relationship, you can find some important resources at the back of this book. Remember, if someone is hurting or touching you without your consent, it's never your fault.

No one is entitled to your body or your time. No one is entitled to say negative things about you or to cross your boundaries. You can check in with your gut feelings if you have a friend who's making you feel bad about your boundaries or choices.

If you don't feel comfortable saying no to someone, or you don't feel comfortable being yourself around them, it's okay to take a step back and think about whether this is a healthy or unhealthy relationship. It's okay to find support.

No one is entitled to your body or your time.

You can take space away from people whenever you need to.

Chapter 6:
But What If...
(Power, Porn, & Unsafe Situations)

We talked about how some people don't have as much agency depending on how much power they have. Power dynamics exist in relationships where someone has more power or control over someone else.

Every relationship can have power dynamics, but they are not always equal. Some examples of relationships with unequal power dynamics are relationships between someone much older and someone much younger, a teacher and a student, or a boss and an employee.

Other unequal power dynamics exist when someone is more popular, has more money, or has more privilege than another person does. When someone has privilege, it means that their identity has not caused people to treat them unfairly. For the person with less power, it can be really hard to change or control their agency, even though having less power doesn't mean they're a weaker person.

Racism, classism, sexism, homophobia, transphobia, ableism and other systemic problems can all impact consent. This is because people with privilege are more likely to be believed and respected if they say something is nonconsensual. (If some of these words and concepts are new to you, go to the glossary to find out more.)

You can always say NO, even to people with more power than you.

Don't touch my hair!

Gender is a big factor in how we think about and learn about consent. There are gendered expectations our society puts on us depending on whether we've been raised as a boy or as a girl. We're often taught that boys are (or should be) assertive and aggressive in pursuing touch with others. This can give people an excuse for bad behavior, which is why some people say things like "boys will be boys." People might even give boys a negative reaction when they're not performing an aggressive gender role.

Girls are sometimes encouraged to think about other people's wants and needs more than their own. They are also sometimes taught that sexual activity is about what they will "allow" a boy to do with them, as the "defender" of their bodies.

If these ideas sound sexist, it's because they are! These ideas also assume everyone will be heterosexual. Ideas like this can harm people of all genders and sexualities because they can make them feel pressured to perform their gender in a way that doesn't align with their own individual wants and needs. Instead, these ideas make them feel like they need to play the role that society tells them to play. That definitely doesn't sound like consent to me!

Sometimes, someone older than you might feel like they can be the boss of your body. They might think their age gives them power over you. Most places have laws called "age of consent laws," where you have to be a certain age to be able to consent to being sexual with another person. These laws are different in different places, but they are in place to help people who are not yet able to consent stay safe.

Kids also can't consent to sending or receiving sexual pictures or videos of any kind. In fact, it's not legal! These laws are in place to protect kids from having images shared without consent.

It's not okay for someone to send you a sexual picture without your consent. If you do receive one, it's not okay to send it to someone else, but you can tell a trusted adult about it. Adults can legally share images consensually, but it's still important for them to be careful when, where, and with whom they share them.

Pornography (or porn) means pictures or videos of people with little or no clothes on, being sexual with themselves and/or other people. People can have different feelings about this. Some feelings are positive and some are negative.

Porn on the internet is not the best way to learn about sexual consent. It's not usually an accurate representation of what sexual activity looks like in real life, and it's very rare that it includes consistent communication or consent between partners.

It's also definitely not for kids! One of your trusted adults can be a good resource if you need help with online safety, or if you want to talk about something you found on the internet that makes you feel uncomfortable.

Some situations can be even more confusing or complicated when it comes to consent. If you ever have a question about what's okay or want to talk about feeling unsafe, it's important to talk about it with a trusted adult.

It can be good practice to talk about a fictional situation and think about what you might feel and what you might do if you were ever in that character's shoes. Your own values and gut feelings might be different from someone else's, so it's extra important to practice communicating about them.

"Does that character on the show look comfortable?"

"Did you hear anyone ask for consent?"

"Wow, they're talking behind his back—how do you think he'd feel about that?"

What should you do if you see something happening that doesn't look consensual? We can choose to be a bystander (standing by to watch what happens) or we can choose to be an upstander (standing up and saying something).

It can be uncomfortable to be an upstander, and in some situations, like if grown-ups are fighting, it can be unsafe. If it's safe to be an upstander, that is a very brave choice to make. There are lots of instances where you might practice being an upstander.

Here are three examples: If someone tells a joke to a group that makes you uncomfortable, you can say, "I don't want to hear that. Does anyone else want to come play ball over there?"

If someone is telling a story about someone else who isn't there, you can say, "Even if that rumor is true, I don't think he would want to be talked about like this."

If someone is doing something that is making others uncomfortable, you can also find an adult to help intervene. Helping to keep people safe is not tattling.

One big reminder: We don't live in a culture that always values consent! We don't live in a culture that prioritizes our own bodies or their needs. To be able to communicate what your body needs, and your body boundaries, you will first need to think about what your needs and boundaries are. Then you can communicate them confidently to others.

It might feel unusual or even unwelcome to others to hear about your boundaries. Even if other people—including adults—react like it's weird or rude to stand up for yourself and your boundaries, it's not!

By claiming your bodily autonomy and your agency over your choices, you're standing up for yourself. You're also showing other people how best to treat you and others with respect. It can sometimes take courage to make consent a priority for yourself and others.

Even if other people don't have practice with consent (or aren't so good at it) you get to use all these skills. You are in charge of your yes and your no!

Chapter 7:
Resources for More Information

This book has a lot of information in it, but there's so much more out there. If you have more questions, I hope you'll be able to talk to a parent, doctor, therapist, teacher, school counsellor, or another trusted adult. There are also many wonderful resources that do the great work of comprehensive sexuality education, providing information, and creating community. Here are some places to go for further education, guidance, and support:

ACLU Guide for Supporting Transgender Students
www.aclu.org/report/schools-transition

Advocates for Youth
www.advocatesforyouth.org

Amaze
www.amaze.org

Bish Training
bishtraining.com

Brook
www.brook.org.uk

Gender Spectrum

www.genderspectrum.org

GLSEN

www.glsen.org

Health for Teens UK

www.healthforteens.co.uk

HRC's Welcoming Schools Foundation

www.welcomingschools.org

I Wanna Know

www.iwannaknow.org

PFLAG

pflag.org

Planned Parenthood

www.plannedparenthood.org

Queer Kid Stuff

www.queerkidstuff.com

RAINN

www.rainn.org

Scarleteen

www.scarleteen.com

Sex Education Forum

www.sexeducationforum.org.uk

Sex, etc.

www.sexetc.org

Sex Positive Families

www.sexpositivefamilies.com

Sexuality Information and Education Council of the United States (SIECUS)

www.siecus.org

Talk With Your Kids

www.talkwithyourkids.org

Teaching Sexual Health

www.teachingsexualhealth.ca

Teaching Tolerance

www.tolerance.org

The YES! Project

yourempoweredsexuality.org

Glossary Words

ableism: unfair treatment and negative opinions against disabled people

affirmative consent: enthusiastic and verbal agreement to participate in sexual activity (yes means yes)

agency: a sense of control and self-directedness; ability to make choices free of constraint

autism/autism spectrum disorder: a kind of neurodevelopmental disorder that can involve differences in or challenges with social skills, repetitive behaviors, speech, sensory input, and communication

boundary: limits and rules about how we would like to be treated in relationships, physically and emotionally

bystander: a person who witnesses a problem behavior and does nothing about it

classism: unfair treatment and negative opinions against people who have less money and wealth

compassion: feeling concern for and desiring to help others who are suffering

empathy: the ability to imagine, understand, and share the feelings or experiences of others

grooming: attempting to form a trusting relationship with a young person in order to manipulate, exploit, or abuse them

homophobia: unfair treatment and negative opinions against gay, lesbian, bisexual, and queer people

network: a group of interconnected people (a safety network is a group of people with whom you might feel comfortable sharing when you need help)

neurodivergent: a person whose brain functions in one or more ways that are outside of "typical"; neurodivergent people may have diagnoses like autism, ADHD, dyslexia, or Tourette's Syndrome, among others

neurotypical: a person who fits into expected norms and standards of brain functioning

nonconsensual: not agreed to by all people involved; without consent

nonverbal: communicating with body language, facial expression, tone, posture, and eye contact, among other cues

pornography/porn: visual or printed materials with sexual activity meant to stimulate sexual feelings

power: the ability to influence or have control over others

power dynamics: the balance or lack of balance of power between people interacting with each other

racism: unfair treatment and negative opinions against people of a certain racial or ethnic group that has less power in our society

respect: the care and honor we show to someone or something considered important; taking care of our impact on other people and things

sexism: unfair treatment and negative opinions against people based on their biological sex; the belief that men are better or superior to other genders

sexual consent: agreement to engage in sexual activity (see Chapter 3 for more)

transphobia: unfair treatment and negative opinions against gender expansive, transgender, and non-binary people

upstander: a person who witnesses a problem behavior and speaks out or acts to intervene

verbal: communicating with words, sentences, and language (voice or written)

Acknowledgments

I owe an unbelievable amount of gratitude to those who helped me bring this second book to life. Thank you is just the start.

To my clients and their families; it is the privilege of a lifetime to be your therapist. I will always be grateful for each of you.

To my early readers, Dr Katelyn Regan, Dr Sophie Fink, and Isy Abraham-Raveson; thank you for your reflections, contributions, and collaboration. I am wowed consistently by your work and your unending generosity. I am grateful to you for helping me with this project through its awkward puberty stage.

To my colleagues, my friends, Robyn and Colette. Thank you for helping me become the clinician, educator, and person that I am.

To Dr Linda Hawkins, Dr Nadia Dowshen, and everyone at the Gender and Sexuality Development Clinic at CHOP, you're still my heroes. Thank you for your work and your ongoing collaboration.

To everyone on the team at Jessica Kingsley Publishers, thank you! David Corey, you just get it. I am so appreciative of your vision and your drive. To Alex DiFrancesco, what a perfect addition to this team. Thank you for your advocacy and camaraderie and for the coffee dates.

To Noah Grigni, the most beautiful person, whose art makes

words sparkle. Your collaboration is a gift and I appreciate it more than you know. Thank you for doing it all again.

To Mom, Dad, Sara, Todd, Josh, and Brandon; I couldn't do any of it without you. I can't begin to express my gratitude for your unconditional love and support. I wouldn't trade you for the world.

To Cait and Kara, my everythings. Your belief in me often precedes my own. Thank you for reading, listening, backing me, and filling my life with the joy of being known so well.

To Andrew, my partner in everything. You're the best champion of my work. Thanks for checking the book reviews, offering your insight, and doing lots of night-nights. The book could not have been if not for you. Thank you for holding it all.

And to Benji, the best creation of them all. You never cease to surprise and amaze. My wish for you is a world where you can discover your own **yes** and **no** with boundless curiosity, safety, and respect.

A special note of gratitude goes to anyone and everyone who read or bought "The Every Body Book"; I hope it helped to facilitate conversations in your family or community. Knowing about your body, mind, and whole self is a **right**. You deserve accurate information, without judgment, to help figure it all out along the way. Let's imagine a better world together, one with widespread liberation and books for everyone.